Leave With More
Than You Came With

by
Christian Hanz Lozada
and
Steven Hendrix

ARROYO SECO PRESS

Arroyo Seco Press
www.arroyosecopress.org

Cover art by Anna Lozada *A Mixed Self*

Author photo by Lessa Kanani'opua Pelayo-Lozada

logo by Morgan G. Robles
morganrobles.carbonmade.com

ISBN-13: 978-1-0954-0726-4
ISBN-10: 1-0954-0726-0

for Lessa

for Erin

for Langston

Contents

"Identity is what we bequeath, not what we inherit, what we invent, not what we remember. Identity is the distorted image in the mirror that we must break the minute we grow fond of it."

-Mahmoud Darwish

"What am I in this place of loss and heartbreak? How do I bear the weight of my soul?"

-Joy Harjo

Why Are We Even Doing This?
Fragmentary Ruins of an Introduction

The book you hold in your hands is like the word aloha carved into the wall of a public restroom: appropriated, well-intentioned, and incorrect. It is written by one and a half white men egging each other on. In other words, we destroy other people's property to express ourselves. In the destruction, though, we start to understand ourselves a bit more; but in the destruction, that understanding falls apart and fails. At their core, these poems are about misunderstanding: misunderstanding identity or an identity misunderstanding, I don't know. I'm not the smart one. They represent our attempt to understand ourselves and how we fit in our world, and that is always a futile gesture. But with each attempt comes the hope to truly understand, even a little, or rather, misunderstand less. We chose to write this book together because we've known each other long enough that we misunderstand each other well. And maybe to destroy each other, finally.

We are an odd pairing visually, emotionally, politically, racially, geographically, sizemically, attitudinally, so why not put the expressions of two disparate people in the same book with no marker to show whose work is whose outside of occasional contextual clues? If you're here for only Steve, good luck. You want to skip to Christian's section? Nice try, pal. In other words, this book goes different routes to get to the same destinations.

Part of my process of learning about myself in the hopes of changing is to appropriate the ruins of others, sift through them, and discover the destruction I've caused. But even more valuable have been the times I've had to sift through my own ruins. A few years ago, Christian gave me a print of Basquiat's *St. Joe Louis Surrounded by Snakes*. The painting haunts me every time I look at it or think about it. While Basquiat was speaking directly to the black experience, as with all great works of art, there are multiple layers of meaning. To be surrounded by snakes is to be embedded in a structure of white power and privilege, a structure my professor Ray Lacoste referred to as The United Snakes of America—nice coincidence, huh? And to complicate matters further, Basquiat's snakes are not exclusively white people, but anyone who acts, even unconsciously, to uphold the status quo of this structure. For a person of color, this structure is painfully apparent every day of their lives. For white people, there is a sense of comfort within a structure that rarely warrants questioning. It took me a while to misunderstand less how my best friend was experiencing this same structure we were both living in. Past misunderstandings destroyed me from within. But in sifting through the ruins, I've discovered a lot about myself.

While these poems deal with many different aspects of identity through the lens of our individual perspectives, many of them question that very structure which has helped to create our identities—again with the hope to decrease misunderstanding and ideally to begin to effect change.

I hated Steve when I first met him. To be accurate, I didn't hate him, but the idea of him. He swooped up the supervisor position I had earned. He ruined my controlling the bookselling world. His presence, not his personality, was my first solid evidence that Borders Books if not America, was not the meritocracy it professed to be, so, in effect, he left America in ruins, too. As time went on, we worked well together. I made him look good, and I looked good by association? I don't know why we became friends other than a general joy to be in his presence. We talked about our worlds:

books and movies. We made up advertisements and monitored data to prove whose campaigns were better, like my "_____ It's Truly The Sport of Kings" signs on a display for each of the sports we had books for. Or his 8 point font sign "These Books Are Hard To Read" for philosophy titles.

The sad thing is I should still hate Steve, not him, but the idea of him. Despite our friendship, despite working well together, he got the professional accomplishments I was envious of despite what, to me, looked like equal amounts of effort. There are the promotions at Borders before I jumped ship after realizing the system was rigged against people of color (You know who agrees with me? Walter Mosley. He chastised Borders during a keynote speech they hired him to give). There's Steve's jump to the corporate world where I floundered in crappy temp jobs before going back to school. There's him actually having a retirement plan whereas my plan is to die of old age in the classroom, not for want but for necessity.

So we are an odd pairing. We both do and don't belong together. I often hear it said that if we look past skin color and where we came from, we are all just human beings underneath. It's a sentiment usually spoken by white people who have the luxury of looking past skin color. I would say, if we don't look past skin color, or where we came from, or our individual heritages, we are still human beings.

We are an odd pairing because the power structures of America are embedded even in our friendship. Steve was my boss when I first met him. He is my boss in writing this book. While he has never acted according to his power over me, it is present, and I bristle at it, not him. Knowing the power dynamic exists but remaining friends shows the work we do to understand each other and ourselves moment by moment.

And the continued presence of unequal power means we must live in the ruins of what could be.

Christian's brown skin, his Filipino heritage, and his white heritage have all gone into making him the human being he is, and he's one of the best human beings I know. That's why we've become such good friends. The best human beings are the ones with the courage to reduce you to ruins and then help you to rebuild... over and over.

This book, this appropriated aloha, should be read by searching through the ruins of two incongruent voices as they try to bridge the painfully dissimilar. And our sincerest hope is to reduce you, the reader, to ruins.

alone with the words

I sit at the small table
trying to understand
what has driven me here
trying to figure out
how to put it into words
and wondering why
it even feels necessary to do so

a feeling of emptiness
tyranny of all forms
an unflagging culture industry
and the overwhelming age of apathy
have left me impotent
unable to take direct action
as I would imagine myself doing
in another time, in another place

so I hide away
take a seat at the small table
call it cowardice
just me and the keyboard and the words
and I start to pound them out
sifting through the ruins of personal history
shaping and unshaping and reshaping identity
peering into the abyss of madness
gazing at the void of hunger and poverty
staring down racism and appropriation
hanging on to the absurd hope
that if I close my eyes
and pound the keys hard enough
the words just might reach you

1

The Lean, Mad Days

and you were worried about stereotypes

my wife and I went to dinner
at Market Broiler in Huntington Beach
she ordered the yellow tail
which seemed to be lacking something
"this needs soy sauce," she said,
"but I don't want to fit a stereotype."

"nobody's going to stereotype you,"
I said, "you worry too much.
people are sensitive to prejudicial thinking
and aren't going to say things
that can have an adverse effect
on relations within certain social settings."
I can sound like a pretentious
asshole sometimes.
"besides," I said, "this isn't
exactly cheap. you might
as well enjoy your food."

when the old,
white waitress
walked by
I stopped her
and asked
if they had
soy sauce
gesturing toward
the fish

4

she looked at my wife
and said they did
and then asked her
if she wanted
a little bowl
to pour it into
"no thank you,"
my wife said
"I'll just pour it
straight on the fish."
"okay," the waitress said.

"do you want chopsticks?"

The Complex Flavor of Kalbi Ribs

Ingredients:
2-3 lbs. short rib beef
You know the kind,
cut across the ribs instead of along,
slim, thin, and perfect blend of fat and cartilage.
2/3 cup soy sauce
>My wife says "Call it shoyu.
>We aren't Chinese."
>"We aren't Japanese either," I say,
>"wait, you are part Chinese."
>"It's called shoyu."

3/4 cup brown sugar
>no
>even as a diabetic's child, I say no.
>2 cups sugar

3 inches fresh ginger
>Contemplate using it in fried chicken instead.

1 garlic clove, minced
>Seriously, fried chicken sounds good, right?

Chop green onions for garnish
>"No," my wife says, "Tutu is allergic to onions."
>Regret and say, "but Tutu is dead."

1 tablespoon sesame oil
>Sometimes substitute with oyster sauce
>to remind the wife of your honeymoon's taste.

You saved money and shared ribs at the local restaurant
where they snuck the real poi to real customers,
where you watched the luau with a local's discount
        from the patio next door,
where you hoped
and hoped
and hoped.

Directions:
Coat meat in sugar until it looks like you.
Don't worry, it already feels like you:
bare, stretched, thin.
Mix remaining ingredients in a bowl
        like you:
                kind of Asian but common
Pour over meat and let mix, mix, mix.

Documentaries Make Me Hungry

You know
the ones about the food industry
you're not supposed to want a big mac afterward,
and I don't.
I want to pause the movie,
speed to a drive through,
and supersize it to go
so I can eat and watch.

Before you think me sick,
I have been to a slaughterhouse
and have seen pigs and goats slaughtered for dinner.
My parents did what their parents did
after the sacrifice
and my horror
they fed me the best parts.

Ferlinghetti: *This is Not a Man,* **1994**

the mask hides terror-stricken eyes
meeting death's stoic gaze
the electrical current frying meat
from the inside out
sizzling like bacon in a pan
smoking like bone in brisket
outpacing the brain's impulses
and the heart's rhythm
blood seeping through
whatever orifice it can find
in this sacrifice without feast

and I won't even mention ~~race~~

Changing Lent

I remember enough from my one year in Catholic school—
before being removed for stealing—
that Lent was all about giving up meat.
That year I learned about it was great!
My family was amazing at Lent.
Dinner was beans and rice, lunch was pb&j,
breakfast was a warm mug of nothing.

Right now, the Christians are screaming at me:
it's about sacrifice, not about meat.
I say unto you, you cannot sacrifice nothing,
you privileged, fuck.
So stop all this bullshit about giving up candy
alcohol
gossip
sex and soda
and see that what you courageously give up
is sometimes a desperate
        lonely
                only
                        spark of joy,
a fleeting light that blinds for hours after a second of clarity.

the lean, mad days

those Long Beach days
those lonely, mad student days
competing with the cockroaches,
foraging for food in the cupboards,
anything I might have missed
every other time I looked.
I yelled out in the direction of the
scurrying, pattering legs on wood and linoleum,
"let me know if you find anything,"
and when I heard the sound fade into the walls
I knew they hadn't found anything either.

In Absence You Grasp at Passing Pieces of Pride

The Years That Must Be Forgotten

With hours on the pier and little patience,
the children find sea gulls to torment
and never stray far from their parents,
their parents and the buckets of dying fish,
fish sometimes too small for bait
but too big to hook whole.
All of us are clothed in the sweat and muck of working days.
Our shirts and pants void of creases
the material hangs too snug
or too loose
from the years of plenty
or the other years.

Memories of Poverty

That anxiety felt even in the shelter of suburbia,
that thought that if even one thing goes wrong,
food will no longer be plentiful,
there will be times when it is absent,
it is then the scavengers are born,
become coyotes wandering the surrounding hills,
and the anxieties transform, become more focused,
the lavender scented bed sheets
are erased from the memory,
along with other frivolities,
and only those memories which provided the most comfort,
those memories which alleviated some of the anxiety,
when something like happiness was experienced,

only those memories remain, come to the fore
even when the reality of hunger
is still a dream experienced
in the shelter of suburbia,

the new anxiety brings those memories into focus
prepares them for the lean years
which may or may not come.

The Square Root of Poverty

If my poverty has a square root,
It is my White Grandma
with her roots that stretch back to Revolution,
roots that never took.

You could call her an orphan
her mom dead
her dad dead drunk,
but unlike her orphanage-bound siblings,
White Grandma was given to the neighbors.

She won't call herself an orphan
because she cried when her new mother
gave her a pair of shoes.
Oh the joy.
Oh the pride.
For some poor, wealth is a healthy family
or a painted house
for others it's a full stomach
for her it's shoes.
She says there is no better foundation than your two feet.

And she won't call herself an orphan
because she cried when her new father
let her go to school.

She cried because her new not-family had roots
deep enough for her to learn rather than work
to read rather than reap
She cried on the way home from school
passing the Jim Crow kids
who wore store bought clothes
and my god, she said, their shoes were gorgeous.
Go tell a history book about White Grandma's tears.
Go tell racism about her envy.
I would say "It's about more than skin, god damn it!"
and think about poverty and economics.
"Yes," she would agree.
"Yes, it's about shoes."

In the absence of heritage, family, money, education,
in the absence of roots,
you grasp at passing pieces of pride,
and White Grandma caught shoes.

To admire them,
though,
she could never raise her head.

Broke History: Mom 2

The Fergusons are nice people
so I'm told
that fill their own Tennessee county
so I'm told.
None of them moved far.
None of them except my grandparents and their kids.
To hear stories of the Fergusons
and Kingsport from Mom's lips
is like listening to longing.
Always joy
always glowing
never about how her husband's dark skin won't let her go home.
never about her father selling his part of the land
never about loss.
The stories of the Fergusons
and Kingsport from Mom's lips
are always present tense.

We're not immigrants anymore

mother tells stories of fat grandma
whom I never met
who spoke little english but enough
to make up for a husband
who refused to learn
a husband who could not find work
because he would not learn
fat grandma who kept the family fed
who kept the family sheltered
who taught the family new world survival

mother tells stories of sunday dinner
of fat grandma feeding the neighborhood
with large pots of spaghetti and meatballs
and plenty of cheap wine
the neighbors could come inside
and sit at the table
and eat and drink and talk together
the homeless
would have to stay outside
and sit on the porch
sit on the steps
and eat and drink and talk together

mother tells stories
around the kitchen table
of her suburban home
where the neighbors
don't know each other
where the neighbors
don't eat or drink or talk together

Hunger Is A Snowflake

I've always been pretty fat,
but my parents have gone without food.
My mom was white-trash hungry,
which means the embarrassment of food stamps
and proving poverty on a bi-weekly basis.
My dad was third-world hungry;
I have no concept of that horror.
Both of them are driven by the ghost of empty stomachs past,
phantom pains that leave scars where no one can see
and have to be proven and disproven on a bi-minute basis.
So growing up, my brothers and I ate,
pathologically, we ate.
Every morning, after Dad's 7pm to 7am shift,
he'd scream into random fast food microphones:
"give me twelb of the cheep ones."
By "cheep" ones, he meant buck menu burgers
sandwiches
tacos
and every morning, like it was Christmas,
we'd wake up and divvy our shares:
half for breakfast and lunch
half for dinner.
To this day, mayo doesn't taste right to me
unless it sits out for a day.

If we had leftovers when Dad woke for work,
he would scream about desperation and sacrifice
about love and devotion
about gratitude and hungry days,
days spent begging family and friends for food.
In response, we would eat and cry,
making the salty burgers saltier,
and hope our tears and gratitude would be enough
to ease his once and always hungry stomach.
If it wasn't,
if he still felt slighted,
he would stop bringing food home
to make us feel what he felt
to make us beg friends at school
for the apples and carrots and celery they wouldn't eat.
I would lie to my Muslim friend about pork in his school lunch.
You see, I never went hungry,
but I've woken up to hunger every goddamn day.

Son of a Scab

Where others were desperate,
my father saw opportunity.
He'd use vacation time,
cross the picket line,
work where others wanted more.
His equation was simple: body + want = desperation,
and his want was constant.

In my first workers' march,
I ignored the opportunity
and looked past the desperation.
What I saw was something simple
beautiful.
I saw generations of workers,
uniting and reuniting,
I saw families be families.
And on a basic level, we were just bodies.

What I learned was, in a world of paper,
the crowd's connections don't matter,
nor do the broken bodies that did the work,
the breaking bodies doing the work,
the bodies that hope there will be work,
or the bodies that filled the march.
What my father failed to learn
was that bodies are only desperation on paper.

St Francis in Boston

Walking down Hanover Street in Boston,
I stopped at the old Catholic church,
built in 1873 by Italian immigrants.

Beautiful statues stood on the lawn
outside the church: St Francis, Mary,
Jesus, and the inside, though small,
had beautiful stained glass windows.

The feeling inside was overwhelming
like any old catholic church, a sense
of awe, of smallness amidst grandeur.

But I was more interested in those who
built the church than the church itself.
Immigrants new to America, speaking
little to no English, living in poverty
in a strange land, needing a place
where they would feel accepted.

Building the church so their families
could have a sanctuary from the racism,
exploitation, deceit. Where they could meet
and be with people who understood them,
who struggled as they did, who had memories
of the old world as they did.

They had chosen St Francis as their patron,
he who knew and understood poverty,
knew the struggle for survival, for acceptance,
knew the old world and its memories,
but had tried to create a new world,
a new community of connectedness,
hope, and compassion

A Lesson on Poverty

I went to elementary school in Compton.
If my parents placed bets on my survival,
they both lost

We were so poor
the thing that kept us going was my dad's job.
Boiler room: skippy dog food
      because we ate dogs or we ate dog food.
          choose your own racist reading
the thing that kept us going was each other
      because we hated each other or we loved each other.
          insert what your family needs

We were so poor we couldn't have good pets.
The place was like the elephant exhibit at the LA Zoo
animals everywhere with no one taking care of them
      pigs, chickens, rabbits, dogs
      it was awful
          I know what you're thinking, those are excellent pets
      Not when you have to eat them
We were so poor,
White mom said I turned brown
because soap and water were too expensive

What I learned about race is that when you're poor,
life is all about hate
you hate the person you are
the place you came from
and the thing you just ate

Something Not One Thing

Phoenix Resting

when war broke out
        and he tried to enlist
    and the army rejected him
            and the navy rejected him
and he was told he could not fight in their war
        he went to the bars
    and he picked fights
        with the soldiers and the sailors
            and told everyone he fought in world war two

when they stripped him of his job
        stripped him of his access badge
            stripped him of his dignity
    he raised his head to look them in the eye
    he raised his fist to look them in the mouth
        he raised his cock to curse them with another generation

when his family had no clothes
    when his family had no shelter
he draped them in the American flag
        he clothed them in hope
            he sheltered them in the dream
        then he wiped their asses with it so they wouldn't forget
        what cloth was for
            what hope was for
                what dreams were for

but at ninety years old
after he watched his wife's memories fade away
after he watched her confined to a circus for the elderly
after he watched her heart explode and her body go limp
     and her ashes spread to the four winds
he lay down his head
     his head on the soft down pillow
          the soft down pillow forming to his head
          the soft down pillow providing a comfort
               he hadn't felt from it before
he lay down his head
     never to raise it again

Tell me again, Nina

Tell me again, Nina, about the sadness
the one that runs deep like rivers
the one I hear reverberate in your voice

Tell me about my history
     the history of America
     the history of sadness
     what made me who I am today
I'm lost, floating in a world between truth & illusion
     between sunshine & earth
     between a blue sky & a black one
     your voice the billion strands of light
          trying to reach me

Tell me again, Nina, about Mississippi goddam
     tell me about the burning buildings
     the burning crosses
     I hear the crackle of fire in your pauses
     I sense the weight of horror
     it's the centuries of ash
          we find ourselves wading through
          drying our throats
               (don't let it dry yours)
          creating our thirst to hear those sad tones

     those who are already dead
     those who will soon be dead
     are ghosts riding your breath
          your breath captured and endlessly repeatable
          yourself a ghost now, haunting my breath

Tell me, Nina, how does time stop
        when I hear your voice
        how does the world melt away
                leaving only sadness
                (and where does the pleasure come from
                that's embedded in the sadness)

Let me embrace you, Nina
        let me embrace your voice
        I'll ride your breath with the ghosts
                and make them my friends
        we'll hold hands until the sadness departs
        and if it never departs
                we'll hold our breaths
                and cover ourselves with ash

It's Pretty Damn Thin

Blood is thicker than water
but it's not the hardest thing to clean.
Patriarchal
Matriarchal
it all comes out in the wash
including blood.
Lineage is a false promise that casts more shade than light
My genealogy and ancestry tests point to a long, proud, white heritage
but that doesn't mean you don't call for back up
because the large
      brown
          man
might react negatively to your rejection
on rejection
on rejection
for nothing reasons
for comparable but . . .
for excessive competence.
Blood is thicker than water
but it ain't as durable as skin.
The darker the skin, the harder the heart works,
under that kind of strain,
it's no wonder so many hearts break.

An Old Italian Custom

is what my mother called it
when a fork, a spoon,
or a salt shaker from the restaurant
found its way to her purse.

My Mom Might Be Racist

My white mother is from the so-poor-Jim-Crow-South
that her school was worse
than the colored school down the road,

but

she worked hard
married an ambitious Filipino,
got her money.

but

money is never enough.
It's as if she's waiting

waiting

for one bonus,
one raise,
one lottery ticket

waiting

waiting to hire a brown boy
named Cletus, Paco, or Chang
waiting for him to serve
mint juleps while tending lawn

but

"Mom," I say.
"Mom, I'm brown, too."

She pats me on the head and says,
"Only on the outside,
son."

See Me.

I wear the skin of a brown man
like the canvas of a mural
that goes on for days and days.
Painted upon by the world's moods
Sometimes more brown
sometimes less.
With every coat of paint, my canvas sags on its frame.
Maybe with the next layer, the wood I call my back
will crack.
If not the next, the next.

But under my skin beats the heart of a White woman,
who weeps for the pain
who relates to being the object
but who does nothing to change it
for fear of losing all that it has gained.

I wish my skin and heart matched
then maybe my words,
created inside and existing out,
would say something untranslatable
but beautiful and true;
SOMEthing but not one thing
but never one thing

I Mourn What I Was

When I hired teens, second-starters, parents, and the bored for
    dead end retail jobs
my idea of leadership was one part connection
      I was looking for scraps of ambition
one part racial discrimination
      I avoided interviewing ethnic-sounding names
Not because of an absence of ambition
but because I didn't want to look like an idiot.
I was looking for the rich in spirit
      Western spirit
I was looking for human beings
      Western human beings

My racism was worse than violent.
What I did was judge before skin
Judge before experience
Judge before birth
I judged the names applicants received
and found their parents' choice wanting.
No,
No, I wasn't violent
but I attacked culture and history and tradition
and while I was looking for connections,
I worked hard to make sure I never made them.

Basquiat: *Untitled (Life Study)*, 1983

the things we carry:
wax wings
melting

I am the sum of my parts
seen and unseen
and subtracted

I am less than my eyes see
I am more than your eyes see

do not dissect me
or create your maps upon me
or think that you can discover me
when I haven't yet discovered myself

The Prompt

"Imagine yourself living 300 or more years. You have the same personality and body. Write a poem about yourself and your interactions with the people of that time."
—some bullshit 30 for 30

I pause in thought.
300 years is too far for me
the concept of it scares and fascinates me
because it's a bit tone deaf.
As a brown man in America, my life's expectancy is diminished.
If the environment doesn't get me, my heart will.
The daily strain of "will it be me?"
"Will it be now?" pulls it to breaking.
The daily pressure of "It wasn't."
"It's later." squeezes the heart to bursting.
Every sign that stays my statistical probability,
every success I celebrate
is tinged with survivor's guilt
for the different me's that weren't allowed
and the me's that were
but didn't deserve it.
So imagine yourself living 300 or more years
with a heart that is smashed daily.
You have the same personality
the same brown body.
Write a poem about yourself and how you survived
and feel good about it.

Everyone Who Visits Takes

Plastic Spatulas Are Traditional Hula Instruments

You have seen her before, the hula dancer,
but only in costume,
swaying her hips as sexual overtures.
To you, her moves are authentic or sensual.
    Exchanged money means you see what you want,
    Just don't ask her to shake her hips
        that's the wrong culture
        and the third act.
But I have seen her holding a plastic spatula.
She flips pancakes and eggs as awkwardly as me.
That's authenticity.
That's sensual.

Because I saw the girl splatter eggs and oil,
I see all the dancers holding spatulas.
All of them smiling,
owning moments with a shared beat,
while I, and you, always misunderstand.

A Lesson on Geography

My wife told me about these instances many times,
it was perhaps my whiteness that prevented me from believing,
that felt it must be overstated,
or perhaps my own guilty suppression of a conscience
that told me I had asked the same questions before of others.
Then I witnessed it myself, could no longer deny,
'Where are you from?" he asked her,
and I saw the change in her eyes
as the question registered
and her eyes caught mine, forcing my recognition,
silently communicating to me,
("you see?")
I blinked in affirmation
or in an effort to erase the question from existence,
erase the pain, past and present.
"Huntington Beach," she replied.

I Don't Feel Like I Look

Jollibee, a fried chicken and spaghetti joint,
with my half-brother's half-Filipino daughter.
She looks at the picture on the wall
of the family eating fried chicken and asks
"Why is that family Asian?"
I answer, "We're in a Filipino restaurant."
"How do you know?"
"Listen."
We hear the singsong Tagalog infix bubble around us.
She asks, "Are we Filipino enough to be here?"
I look at the fair skin on the wall and realize:
I, like my niece, do not feel this place is home,
do not see myself in the family picture,
cannot be part of a family that complete.

"Probably not."

I Am Something I Am Not

At a popular Italian restaurant in old San Juan Capistrano
I see pictures on the wall of famous Italian American athletes:
Joe DiMaggio, Mike Scioscia, Rocky Marciano,
a young Tony Danza with his boxing gloves,
and the obligatory Sylvester Stallone as Rocky Balboa,
Dean Martin and Frank Sinatra are singing overhead.
I imagine what pride the owner must feel in those who broke
     through the barriers,
who struggled for acceptance, represented the others who
     kept struggling;
a pride I was never going to feel
because my family struggled so hard to fit in
that they let go of all that connected them to the culture.

For a moment I try to feel the owner's pride
until he comes out of the kitchen,
introduces himself to my brother,
asks if we're enjoying everything.
My brother engages him,
learns that his parents immigrated from Greece,
that they thought Italian food would sell better,
and opened this restaurant sixty years ago.

The Day Before Relocation

she placed the chemise in the suitcase,
closed the top and buckled it,
she wrapped the vase in newspaper
and placed it in the wooden crate.
then she removed it and unwrapped it.
she paced the length of the living room,
her bare feet making imprints in the carpet,
"why aren't you helping me," she said.
"stop," he said. "it doesn't matter"
"what we leave behind will scar us," she said,
"what we take will define us"
"it's too late," he said,
"we've already been defined."
a tear formed at the corner of her eye,
she blinked to force it out, then wiped it away.
"definitions change over time," she said to herself,
"and context is everything."

Hoarders of Hawaii

Ask them
Ask them why keep the pictures
the trinkets?
Ask them why the furniture
the food?
Ask them, and in a language that is
English and Hawaiian,
Portuguese and Japanese
They will answer with need
and loss.
They will answer with foresight,
regret,
and the word: keep.

Keep in mind that cousins bombed
uncles ran the internment camps
spouses were the overthrow.
Keep.
Keep in mind that Hawaii was late to private property
and everyone who visits takes.

Take What You Can Carry
"All Japanese persons, both alien and non-alien, will be evacuated
from the above designated area by 12:00 o'clock noon Tuesday, April
7, 1942."
—from a sign posted in store windows in San Francisco

There was a storm that night
or maybe the storm had already passed
or maybe the storm was those days you were talking about

the clouds gathered in your chest
the moment I asked about your parents' garage
everything piled in mounds
with almost nowhere to step
like a cataclysm had happened

and lightning shot from your eyes
when you told me one had happened
one had happened more than once
a cataclysm
since this world began
this world that began on Angel Island
three and four generations ago
one happened the moment the ships docked
and it lasted for months in some cases

and one happened again
the day they bombed Pearl Harbor
and executive order 9066 was issued
and signs went up in the store windows
and the Terminal Islands were emptied out
and the Tanforans and the Santa Anitas were filled up
and people slept in stables
where the horses used to shit

and one happened again
the day the trains pulled into Minidoka
and Heart Mountain and Tule Lake
and the men checked "no"
and then checked "no" again
because they refused to fight
for a country that wouldn't fight for them

people experience one every day

you said

and thunder burst in my ears

you try being told
you can take only
what you can carry

you said

see how it feels
to decide what to hold on to
what to let go of

and then see if you can
make that decision

again

you looked at me as though
I was a sign in a window
as though the evacuation notice
were written on my face

Living the Hindsight of The Hawaiian Queen's White Husband

If I could stop being a tourist
and turn away all tourists
If I could call back the U.S. forces
and kill the need for armies
If I could make Hawaiian votes count
and make all voices heard
If I could recognize Hawaiian sovereignty
and enforce all treaties
If I could give Hawaiians credit for Hawaii's discovery
and call the new world your world
if
and if
and if

But I need the opposite of "if" to make you
You need what "is" to meet me
that's how it works in oppression,
your love is used against you
"Is" doesn't start with violence,
"is" starts with heart.

Manzanar 1944

My country 'tis of thee
sand, settling like dust upon clenched eyelids,
settling in the crevices of clenched teeth, settling in the
    crevices of clenched souls;
Sweet land of liberty
guards, watching from their looming towers,
watching with their guns pointed inward, watching those
    they're protecting;
Of thee I sing.

Land where my fathers died
sons, departing for the war, to sacrifice themselves for their
    country,
to sacrifice themselves for their family, to sacrifice themselves
    for their unborn children;
Land of the pilgrims' pride
homes, emptied of their occupants, of their owners,
emptied of furniture to be auctioned off, emptied of hopes
    and dreams;
From every mountainside
barbed wire, twisting along acres of fence, piercing outward
    looking eyes,
eyes looking toward the future, left to wonder with the
    wonder of torn flesh,
bleeding, seeping into the desert, into the soil, into the sand.
Let freedom ring!

High School International Day

It's student driven
and resoundingly Asian American
with Pacific Islanders for flair.
The kids sit on the edges of the basketball court—
the stage—
prone, waiting, hungry.
In groups, they share their dances,
flashing their cultural garb,
and it's chaos.
Too many cultures,
too many dances,
too many kids,
and not enough time,
never enough time.

And while they share dances with the audience
I start to notice:
the kids don't change costumes
they don't stay with their groups,
the martial arts display gives way to Bollywood
and karate gi pepper a sari line up,
the sari start to twirl with flamenco skirts,
which then sway with the hula dancers
and all of it is centered with the deep drum and base of
EDM. Leave it to the kids to ignore cultural lines
and choose anarchy over uniformity.

But choose isn't the right word;
thematic moves from one culture to the next are accidents
and weirdly unavoidable.
There is no choice here, no thought
other than the mad dash of togetherness,
the bright and fleeting spark of young, active bodies
before feeling the reins around your neck,
imperceptible
at first
but,
with each turn on the stage,
the slack disappears
a little bit more
a little bit more
a little bit more.

We're Just Looking For Answers

Nani and I walk around an ancient Hawaiian temple.
The strong winds smash against the sides of the lava rock walls,
chasing humor and joy across the plains.
"Do not climb on the rocks," the signs say.
"Do not wrap rocks in Ti Leaves."
I point and ask, "How will I get my wish?"
She pauses and looks at a small enclosure of stacked stone
at a portrait of a middle-aged man propped in the corner
wreathed in rotting flower lei.
She says, "You're an asshole."

The rushing wind is muted inside the walls,
leaving just us and ghosts of people like us.
In the cubbies and other enclosures
we see other offerings:
Shoes.
    Longing.
Alcohol.
    Absence.
An asshole's ti-leaf rock.
    Silence.
And a new crib.

At this last artifact, we leave the heau
and return carrying leaves, lei,
and hearts heavy with hope.

Broke History: Mom 3

Who wouldn't speak
lovingly of rural living
of worlds past
if you move from Tennessee hills
to dingy downtown Long Beach, California.
Old, rooted American
for transient America,
a fixed home
for eviction notices
and poor kids that knew this as normal.
I don't mean to make this about race,
but those poor kids were black.
Think about it:
you're poor, struggling,
white in a black neighborhood
so white the welfare office don't think you need assistance,
so white you should own America
and you don't.
I don't mean to make this about race,
but poverty warps what you hope to be.

Basquiat: *Untitled (Black Tar and Feathers)*, 1982

violent heritage brought forth from slavery past
tar stuck to the canvas as it was stuck to flesh
ripping and tearing it from history without fully separating it
a visceral reminder of a horrifying punishment
the feathers and halos turn martyrs to angels
for us in the present looking back
trying to understand America *now*
how we got here from there
Basquiat reminds us that tarring and feathering
still exists in symbolic America
juxtaposing the past and present
because that's what artists do

arrows of outrageous fortune fall on us
as legacy as heritage from our own hands
we find ways to negotiate with ourselves
to exonerate from blame from willing participation
we haven't tarred and feathered anybody
but there it is staring us in the face
a mirror held up to the depths of our souls
and we see the blackness we can't deny it
though we try
not us but the black hand of fate that has done this
and we're stuck in tar, baby, missing the train
traveling underground along the OHAYO river

I Hear You, Sam Clemens

I've followed you in writing
from the almost unreadable
to the actually unreadable
to the works that give me chills.
Even now, talking to Britt at your graveside,
I have chicken skin
as if you're standing behind me as I'm talking shit about the
    end of Huck Finn.
But it's not the shit talk that resurrects you,
it's not you that I feel,
it's the honesty in Huck seeing another person,
as a person,
for the first time.

I've sat on your rock in Hawaii
where you said you ate with a savage chief
and where some white kid "How"ed for a picture,
cementing blindness with memory and evidence.

I've even tried to continue your stories from Nigger Jim and
    Injun Joe's points of view
because your sight is restricted by the colors its shaded in
and mine is a different shade than yours
and from a different angle

Treading in your footsteps takes planning, precision,
more time and money than I have,
but I only stumbled on your grave, driving through Elmira,
10 minutes before closing.

Two pens are at your altar already,
making my pencil mean less,
But I think that's how you'd want it,
the grandeur diminished by the accidental.
Someone who has traveled to the most isolated point in the Pacific
to sit on a rock
has to make an illegal U turn
and risk getting kicked out
to visit.
And the sad thing is, I don't see you, Sam,
not really.

The Negro Speaks of Rivers
And a White Man Listens
—for Langston Hughes

I know of rivers:
I know of rivers because I have heard black men speak of
     them, I have heard Native Americans sing of them.

My soul stretches itself to imitate the depth of rivers, so I can
     understand the soul of black and brown folk.

White folks try to sound the depths of rivers without wading in,
Try to measure, quantify with instruments and accept the results,
Their low marks continuing to make the soul of black and brown
     folk grow deep like
          rivers, grow beyond mark twain, mark ta-ree, mark four.

Self-delusion is embedded deep in the souls of white folks.

I know of rivers:
     I have heard tell of a man crossing the River Jordan to
freedom only to be hunted
          down like a rabid dog and returned to his lawful
owner;
     I have heard tell of a trail of tears that left women and
          children who could not
               keep pace drowning in the Mississippi River;
     I have heard tell of Chinese laborers building a railroad
          across the Missouri River
               to support locomotives on which they would
               not be allowed to travel;

59

I have heard tell of a fictitious yellow peril on our
        western shore which led
                toward the Gila River.

I know of rivers that are still deep:
        Seventy percent of prisoners in America are not white,
        Reservations are not considered prisons,
        Literacy is as much about color as it is about language,
        Employment is as much about color as it is about skill.

Self-delusion is embedded deep in the souls of white folks.

Enough Already

Here's another one,
spouting about oppression
with an explanation of race
before a poem about color.
As if I don't get it.

But I do get it.
You live a life different from mine
and need to tell it.

no one's faulting that.

but how would you like it,
living without a culture to call your own?
No twerk or orange chicken
No great migration or holocaust
I mean,
Where is my taco bell?
I do get it.
I do.
The world is racist.

But why beat a dead horse?
At least you've got the stories,
while I am left to create a me
without so much culture.
I mean,
where is the white panda express?

Basquiat: *Native Carrying Some Guns, Bibles, and Amorites on Safari*, **1982**

gazing at a Basquiat
visionary black profit of history
history being now
history being rewritten
before our gaze
he gazes back
as the savage gazes
or rather the savage is gazed upon
in an accusatory manner
you are the cause of this
whether an active participant
or one merely gazing
as a silent partner
as though international corporations
the hunters of fertile soil
crossing lines
to plant their money trees
were so many animals on safari

look out!

~~dis~~cover the truth of colonialism©
the truth that we are kin
the truth that $kin has value

dismantle power structures
through images of malignant illusion
expose the myth of the noble missionary
appropriate appropriation of the crown
given to the griots who lift the veil
allow us to peek behind
but don't tell us what to say
don't provide us with meaning
allow us to determine for ourselves
self-determination

Good ~~God~~!

we know better than you
it's for your own good
we're only thinking of you
when we're wealthy everyone is better off
follow us to the promised land
read this book and follow its ways
it speaks the truth of history
we are all ~~God's~~ children
same old shit

embarrassment of riches
created through ~~class~~ struggle

and I won't even mention ~~race~~

Basquiat: *The Death of Michael Stewart*, 1983

The death of Edmund Perry, 1985
The death of Nicholas Heyward Jr, 1994
The death of Amidou Diallo, 1999
The death of Malcom Ferguson, 2000
The death of Patrick Dorismond, 2000
The death of Prince Jones, 2000
The death of Earl Murray, 2000
The death of Timothy Thomas, 2001
The death of Ousmane Zongo, 2003
The death of Orlando Barlow, 2003
The death of Michael Ellerbe, 2003
The death of Timothy Stansbury Jr, 2004
The death of Aaron Campbell, 2005
The death of Ronald Madison, 2005
The death of James Brissette, 2005
The death of Henry Glover, 2005
The death of Sean Bell, 2006
The death of DeAunta Terrel Farrow, 2007
The death of Oscar Grant, 2009
The death of Victor Steen, 2009
The death of Aaron Campbell, 2010
The death of Steven Eugene Washington, 2010
The death of John T Williams, 2010
The death of Derrick Jones, 2010
The death of Alonzo Ashley, 2011
The death of Kenneth Chamberlain, 2011
The death of Ramarley Graham, 2012
The death of Sgt Manuel Loggins Jr, 2012
The death of Dante Price, 2012
The death of Wendell Allen, 2012
The death of Tamon Robinson, 2012

The death of Kendrec McDade, 2012
The death of Timothy Russell, 2012
The death of Chavis Carter, 2012
The death of Ramarley Graham, 2012
The death of Kimani Gray, 2013
The death of Larry Eugene Jackson Jr, 2013
The death of Clinton Allen, 2013
The death of Dontrell Stephens, 2013
The death of Jonathan Ferrell, 2013
The death of Jordan Baker, 2014
The death of McKenzie Cochran, 2014
The death of Dontre Hamilton, 2014
The death of Eric Garner, 2014
The death of John Crawford III, 2014
The death of Michael Brown, 2014
The death of Victor White III, 2014
The death of Tyree Woodson, 2014
The death of Ezell Ford, 2014
The death of Dante Parker, 2014
The death of Akai Gurley, 2014
The death of Kajieme Powell, 2014
The death of Tamir Rice, 2014
The death of Rumain Brisbon, 2014
The death of Jerame Reid, 2014
The death of Tony Robinson, 2015
The death of Nicholas Thomas, 2015
The death of Philip White, 2015
The death of Eric Harris, 2015
The death of Walter Scott, 2015
The death of Freddie Gray, 2015

Throwing Stars

in the form of a bat,
long tined
four or more points,
it doesn't matter.
When they come on screen, I catch my breath.
They hold as much fascination for me as a gun
because their ranged-danger carries memory.
The alley behind our house in Compton,
a door so full of holes you couldn't tell what color it had been.
In the afternoons, every day, Dad would send us to that door
throwing stars in hand,
and tell us to practice.
We practiced performative culture.
The stars were Asian, not our kind of Asian,
but the Black kids in the neighborhood didn't know the
        difference
so our sessions fired their imaginations of ninja training
        camps
where we double punched the air in unison while making
high pitched whoops
where we scared ourselves with rites of passage.
That door stayed in the alley all day and night,
a reminder and sign not to enter the temple,
and if the warning wasn't enough,
every afternoon, four boys would launch star after star
into it as if it were a black intruder.
Hour after hour, you could hear the muffled thump bounce
        about the walls that separated us
                and them
thump
thump
thump
a lullaby and security blanket to put my dad to sleep before
the graveyard shift.

Seen in All the Ways You Don't Want to Be

The Resounding Silence

six million dead
never again we said
six million dead
never again we said
six million dead
in the Congo
and not a word

Mixed Race Luck

White Grandma says she doesn't see me as brown
she just sees me as me.
I say "the brown makes me who I am
and not seeing it means you don't see me."
"I can't," she says.
"You can't," I say.
"Why don't you want to be white?"
White mom asks.
"I am white."
"But you just made your grandma cry saying she can't see
        you because you're brown."
"I'm both."
She shakes her head,
silently saying she doesn't see me either.
It's the luck of the mixed race:
to be invisible to the people that love you the most
to be seen in all the ways you don't want to be.

The Fighter

My cousin and I sat
at the kitchen table
in our grandparents' mobile home.
We were twelve and ten
and didn't care about our
grandfather's stories
but that never stopped him
from telling them.
He sat in his chair watching the tv
a boxing match
no one famous
because it wasn't pay-per-view
just two young kids
with nothing to lose
exchanging blows
because there was nothing else
to do
because they liked the way
their opponents' soft flesh
accepted their gloved hands
they liked the sound of leather
connecting with the skin
and the bone behind it
and people liked watching
got some sort of satisfaction
out of seeing two barely grown men
knock each other around
until only one was left standing

or until they both valiantly made it
to the end of the twelfth round
proving themselves true warriors
even though only one would
be declared a winner.

"I used to be a boxer," my grandfather said
and you could see the tinge of pride
as the words came out of his mouth.
you could see he had been transported
back to some earlier day
when he had the physical strength
and the stamina
to go toe to toe with any fool who would dare.
"I had this one fight with Rusty O'Dell,
boy could he throw a punch
that dirty bastard
they don't make them like Rusty O'Dell anymore
I wonder whatever happened
to that no good s. o. b.
went the distance with him
and did we ever give it to each other
he was a lefty
hard to fight a lefty
he caught me a couple times
square on the jaw, boy
but I gave him hell too.

those were the days
all you boys are too soft these days
not willing to throw a punch
because you're too afraid to take one."
"I'm a girl, grandpa," my cousin said.
"Hell, I'm not talking to you,
I'm just saying you boys in general
no one wants to get in the ring anymore
unless they're getting paid for it.
we did it for a couple beers ."
my cousin and I sat in silence
not really sure how to respond
feeling a little as though we had
already failed at life because
we weren't alive when it mattered.

"that son of a bitch was never a boxer,"
my grandmother yelled from the other room.

I guess it's easier to just do white

Being of a post-assimilation
italian american generation
on my mother's side
I had very little connection
to the culture
other than some foods
I grew up with as a child
lupini, cannoli, pasta

my father's side
was anybody's best guess
perhaps some german or austrian
perhaps some english or welsh
safer to just say "white"
they had been here longer
and it was harder to tell
where they originated from

so I decided to embrace
my italian american identity
learn about the culture
the struggles people
like my great grandfather
faced speaking almost
no english

I wrote a story
about my grandparents
thinly veiling the characters
with italian sounding
names
and submitted it
to Italian Americana
which had claimed
to publish John Fante
I would become
the next great
italian american writer

my manuscript was returned
with a handwritten
note across the top
"sorry, we only accept
stories and poems
by italian americans"

In Another Life

I would change nothing.
How can I not love my clean streets
when I've lived in littered ones?
How can I not love my education,
when we lied about our address to avoid the local schools?
How can I not love my parents,
        who are more familiar with 7pm-7am shifts
than my birthdate,
        with overtime pay and nighttime differential
than what I write about,
        with lateral moves and promotions
than my month on the badminton team
        before I quit.
                I didn't want to ask for money.
How can I not love Mom
for being Revolutionary white
and non-revolutionary poor?
How can I not love Dad
for being fresh off the boat brown?
How can I not love them for bucking geography, generations,
        governments?
Such struggles stiffen joints
break backs
crush hearts.

In another life, I would change nothing
other than the world.
I would make it so parents could be present,
so that trade—
crushed hearts for cash—
is never on the table
because it's always right
and always wrong.

November

November has come again
and with it loose memories
of an emotional landscape
that time has preserved
in that constant flow
of the seeming everlasting
November has come again
and with it the dulled heartache
of years of mourning
of years of searching the starlit
nights for a phantom spirit
to hush the murmurs of dread

November once found us sitting around the nursing home table
watching my grandmother waste away before our eyes
seeing the terror in hers as she struggled to understand
what had happened, was happening, would happen to her
her memory mostly departed like a gentle, light November breeze
with flashes of lucidity like lightning bolts on a chilled
    Autumn evening

November once found us sitting in my uncle's garage on
    election day
while he lay lifeless in his bed, a gaunt frame of the man he
    had been
even just hours before, and the bustle surrounding us that day,
the hope for renewal in a country that had lost itself, didn't match
those feelings of shock and utter hopelessness that comes
with the hardened grief of losing a father, grandfather, uncle
    so early

November has come again
and with it the layers of dust
from the endless California summer
covering everything
and the one day of rain
that turns it all to mud
and we wander through the mud
unable to imagine how anything
could wash it away, clear our path

November found us again with a mother just returned from
    the hospital
after an infection that spread throughout her body,
    indistinguishable at first
from her normal pain, prevented her from moving, from
    sitting up,
from leaving bed, relying on nurses to change her, unwilling
    to eat anything
as we watched her shrivel to near nothingness, her voice
    barely audible
weeks in a rehabilitation center learning to walk with
    atrophied muscles
training her stomach to accept food again when it seemed so
    foreign now

November found us with a brother rushed to the hospital
    with flu-like symptoms
rushed to emergency surgery to implant stints so dialysis
    could begin immediately
severe dehydration causing kidney failure. . . kidney. . .
    failure
waiting in the same room in the same hospital that mother
    had just left

fear of death constantly in the forefront of the mind
uncertainty driving us to the edge of madness, always the
    uncertainty
considerations of god again, when it seems there's nothing left
    but to pray

November has departed again,
leaving a wake of devastation
but we look toward spring
and the birth of a child
with a chance for new joy
in the midst of November's ruins.

A Spring That Never Comes

(re)collection

identity is a collection of memories and perceptions
filled with gaps

every memory is a metaphor
of the past and present at the same time

every memory is an arrangement of shapes and colors
on a four dimensional surface

every perception is a knife that slices memory
into a thousand minuscule fragments

every perception is a needle and thread
that stitches memory back together

the same memory is different each time it is perceived

time is a ghost that haunts every memory and perception

dementia is a collection of memories and perceptions
wearing masks and haunting time

filled with gaps

"who is Frank Beaver?" my grandmother asks

"that's your husband," my brother says

"oh, that son of a bitch?"

January 28, 1986

I.

I remember running
    in from the playground
    after the morning bell rang
I remember lining up
    at the classroom door
    the same as every day
I remember waiting
I remember
    waiting and waiting
I
remember
waiting
and waiting
and
waiting

It was out of the ordinary
for Mrs. Easterly
our always punctual
fifth grade teacher
to keep us
    waiting. . .
        waiting. . .
            waiting. . .

"I have some terrible news,"
she said
when she finally
opened the door
TERRIBLE NEWS

"come in"

I don't remember
    what she said
    after that

II.

I remember sitting
    at my desk
    in our fifth grade classroom
I remember silence
    as she turned on the television
"I have terrible news"
she said
"come in"

now
I remember
what she said
after that

after we waited…
    and waited…
        and waited…

"the Challenger has exploded"
TERRIBLE NEWS
"children," she said
the Challenger has exploded
someone gasped

I don't remember
who

III.

 I remember watching
        the television
        in our classroom
I remember seeing
        the image
        over and over
TERRIBLE NEWS
the image
        of the rocket booster
        separating
the image
        of a cloud
        of white smoke

the sound
        of cheers
I remember hearing
        the sound of cheers
someone gasped
        maybe the whole crowd
the rocket booster
        separated
the rocket booster
        is supposed to separate
cheers
then a gasp
a collective gasp

something went wrong

IV.

I remember seeing
        fire
I remember seeing
        smoke
white smoke
too much smoke
streamers of smoke
        falling from the sky

TERRIBLE NEWS
something went wrong
gasp
the Challenger has exploded
TERRIBLE NEWS
come in
children

remember this day
remember
        waiting
remember
        fire
remember
        smoke
remember
        gasp

Broke History: Dad 8

Last year, I read a study about diabetes
unbalanced sugar levels
and schizophrenic behavior.
I sincerely hope
that explains a lot about Dad when I was younger.
Think of working graveyard shifts at a dog food plant:
smell the stages of rotting, processing meat
     you puked the first week.
hear the chunk and whir and drone of the boiler room
     communicate in hand signals.

Now go home to kids you don't want.
Drink a coke and eat a candy bar, make it a nightly meal.
It's the least you deserve,
right?

Sometimes the only way to redeem my father
is to pray it was the diabetes.

Broke History: Dad 18

I used to wish Dad is not my father.
My wife and I even joke with Mom
about the Samoan dude she had a crush on,
the one that I look like
because I'm tall for a Filipino
darker than my family,
but when I nursed my cuts and bruises
dished out by abusive brothers
as a reaction to an abusive father
I dreamed
wanting to wake in the middle the night
and slitting their goddamned throats.
Right now you're thinking, "Oh my god!"
but let me tell you,
this is my heritage.
Dad's mother used to wake her children with a pinch
and cold, sharp steel.
My aunts and uncles share this fact and laugh.
I laugh, too.
"Oh, diabetes."

A Circus for the Elderly

A place of dirt and decay
A place of neglect and forsakenness
The first time we were all there together
To celebrate the birthday of the woman we'd abandoned
The woman we'd given up responsibility for
And my brother made a pumpkin pie
Even though she didn't eat anymore
Because pumpkin was her favorite
We knew the pie would be for us
It felt like we were celebrating her life
As though she were already dead
And maybe in a sense she was already dead
The grandmother we had known was no longer there
And this woman who looked like her
Sat and stared at the pumpkin pie
And then she asked for a piece
Surprising the hell out of us all
And she ate it while we all talked around her
As though she wasn't there
And every now and then she would look at the pie
And ask who made it and say it looked good
And she would ask for a piece
As if she hadn't had one yet
And when half the pie was gone
We began to wonder if she was tricking us
If the whole damn dementia was a ruse
If she had abandoned us
Rather than the other way around
Until we remembered where she was
Remembered the dirt and decay
Remembered the neglect and forsakenness
Realized that any functional memory
Would not accept a place like this

A grandmother with dementia remembers

the days are black clouds that won't burst
the flowers all bloom at the wrong time
they don't wait for spring anymore
and the colors don't seem as bright as they once did

they won't let me out of this wheelchair
I thought it would be fun to ride around
I wanted my father to push me
now I don't know where he went
and these people I don't know tell me I can't
I can't get up and walk around
I can't go outside the gate
I can't go home
I can't see my father
I don't want to eat but they tell me I have to
I have to take a bath
I have to change my clothes
I have to comb my hair
I have to go to bed

the metallic taste in the air won't go away
my tongue is swollen with atomic buds

I have a brother
I have three brothers
they're all dead
I never got to say goodbye

I have three children
wait
I have a sister
what happened to my sister?
I said goodbye to her
I remember saying goodbye

I have three children
one is sick
one comes to see me all the time
one gives me whatever I want
a free spirit always

the sonic tension does strange things to my mind
the cells don't all communicate with each other

Christmas 1924 I remember like it was yesterday
I know I don't remember much anymore
I know I remember things like they were yesterday
that didn't happen yesterday
I know the people that come here are my family
even when I don't remember them
I know something is wrong with me
I know I don't have much time left here
and I think I'll be glad when I'm gone
this has become too much
Christmas 1924 I remember like it was yesterday
and I want every day to be like that day from now on
from now on until it ends

my mother bought me the dress we saw in the window
in the window at Macy's in New York City
the last Christmas we spent in New York
before moving to Los Angeles
it was the first time I'd received a dress that nice
it was so I'd have something nice for my First Communion
it was the first time I'd felt that feeling
I don't know how to describe it
but it was in my chest
it was in my hands
it was in my feet
I didn't want it to end
Christmas 1924 I remember it like it was yesterday
I remember the feeling
even though I don't feel it now
and haven't felt it in a long time
I remember the faces around me
my mother's, my father's, my brothers', my sister's
I remember
        I remember
            I remember

the days are white clouds that burst too soon
the flowers don't bloom any more
they wait for a spring that never comes
and the colors are nothing but a temporary memory

That Old Dance

tourists want to see the exotic,
tight skin,
sensual swaying,
they want to see images of the impossible
near enough to touch.
but what's missing at commercial luau
is the kupuna, the elders, dancing.
their arms arthritically slow
their skin brittle
their movements full of grace.
Age tells a story that youth can't
no matter the mele, the song,
and their rhythm makes all stories
familiar.

Sifting Through the Ruins

Flip a coin

Heads I win, tails you lose, you say
and it happens too fast for me to catch the trick
you lift your hand to reveal the quarter
Tails, you lose
and I sit back in stunned silence
as I watch things taken from me
one by one over the next thirty years

Breathing in Reverse
or twelve parts grief

I. A two-year-old sees a mirage

"Daddy."
"That's not your daddy.
That's a black man walking down the street."
"Daddy."
"That's not your daddy.
That's a black man playing basketball in the park."
"Where is Daddy?"
"Your daddy is the wind that blows through you briefly
and carries pieces of you away with it quickly,
the cold that grips your bones, pulls at them,
almost knocking you down,
the absence felt in the deepest recesses of your soul
and crawling through the deepest pores of your skin."
"Daddy will come back."
"No. Your daddy will never come back."
"Daddy will come back."

II. Borrowed time

We return to the site of my birth
St Mary's Hospital in Long Beach
to wait patiently, to wait impatiently
while my uncle undergoes surgery
to remove a basketball-sized tumor
from his liver, hoping, praying,
that it would not be the site of his death.

And we grip tight the rosaries the nuns have loaned us
and we recite cautiously the words the nuns have loaned us
Hail Mary full of grace, the lord is with thee
because it seems the right thing to do in this place.

And my cousin prays her grandfather will not leave her, too,
and she makes promises to God that she knows she cannot
keep, and it works, or something works,
because the doctors tell us he will live,
and we don't know at the time it will only be for ten more
years, and at the time ten more years would have seemed a
long time, and now it doesn't seem long at all.

III. The poet thinks he defines grief

Grief is snow melting on mountaintops
    when all it wants to do is remain frozen;
Grief is a raindrop falling from a cloud
    before it has a chance to say goodbye;
Grief is a ray of sunshine stopped by the shutters
    before it can reach the rhododendron;
 Grief is the watch that stops, never to be wound again;
    the gallows erected and never used;
    the gallows erected and then used;
    the match that breaks;
    the match that burns down the house;

the sum of the distance
between the sun,
the moon,
and the star
that flickered out two million years ago;

probably.

IV. For love of animals

My uncle buys a dog.
She farts and makes him laugh,
she licks his face and makes him laugh,
something none of the rest of us could ever get away with.

V. For love of cars

My uncle buys a Porsche.
He races against death.
He loses, but he loves the race.

VI. The poet reacts to his uncle's death

I unclench my fists,
take a deep, unnatural breath,
pause
then clench my fists again.
I have no words.

VII. A grown child dreams in reverse

Her mother and father are reunited,
she lies cradled in her father's dark arms,
her mother's pale hand runs
through her silky, straight hair that has never
been doused with tear-creating chemicals.
She doesn't look like a little boy in this dream,
she isn't mixed by her race in this place,
she doesn't question her identity here,
she knows who she is, she is a daughter,
but only here, only now, in this moment.

VIII. The poet contemplates grief
in the dead form of the sonnet

Does the tree mourn the leaf that separates
in dry detachment from its limb's embrace
riding the air with an elliptic grace
having achieved every living creature's fate;
or does it celebrate through the lens of dim
remembrance the vibrant green shimmering
against the strands of time, dance and sing
in the crisp breeze a soulful dirge less grim
than the somber notes of abandonment;
does the soil speak through the root a word
of reassurance knowing the fallen leaf
will become the song of a future spring sent
echoing through ages by the chirping bird;
or does it share my cryogenic grief?

IX. For love of humans

She whines as the body bag is carried down the stairs,
she whines as the body bag is carried from the home,
she nudges it with her nose as it passes, tries to follow it,
paces along the path it has taken, and whines long
after it is gone.

The goddamn dog
knows how to grieve
better than I do.

X. Dishes still need to be washed

My cousin presses the sponge hard
along the surface of the ceramic plate
the tips of her fingers turning red
long after the remnants of food
and bacteria have disappeared
and long after the last tear has dried.

XI. The poet contemplates his own mortality

I stand in front of the bathroom mirror
washing my hands in the sink
the warm water running over them
I stare at my face and look for signs of age
I stare at my face and look for signs of my uncle
I stare at my face and look for signs of life
the water continues to run.

XII. The prodigal father returns

We stand in front of the incinerator
as my uncle is placed inside,
the flames jumping out and chilling our bones,
a cold so deep that it makes us stumble without moving,
we hold our coats tight to our bodies,
grip our hearts, our heads, our tears, our grief
to keep them from blowing away
as the winds kick up leaves and ash and particles of earth
that wash over us, cleanse us of our purity.
My cousin looks over at me,
"See, I told you he would come back."

Summer Night Hide and Seek

I remember how,
in Compton we covered ourselves in dark colors
shied from the working street lamps
lingered nearer the posts with blown-out bulbs
to become invisible to our parents calling from doorways and
    windows,
to the world and the seekers.
For safety, we learned to clothe ourselves in layers of dark.

We played for escape,
escape from hot, box-fan houses
from parents with quick, hot hands
from a world where others dictated how you should act
or not
what you should say
or better yet, don't open your fucking mouth at all.
We played for escape from our lives

because being found meant a hard slap on the arm or back
and did not mean the round was over;
it meant your life was.
It meant you could not control your invisibility.

Eventually

you would always get caught
and you'd never see it coming.
They would catch you and replace that freedom of the dark
that safety in being unseen
and return you to your place in that house
with those parents and teachers and bosses
whose frustration burned bright at being caught, too.

Nocturne IX

it's lonely on the edge of night
I don't know if you're still sleeping
in the next room
or if you're a ghost
trapped inside the walls

night used to be the time
we loved each other
now it's the time
we haunt each other

and insomnia is the friend
who won't leave at a respectable hour
who we feel obligated to entertain
who doesn't pick up on our cues
that on the inside
we're slowly splintering

Facebook Stalking

I'm sorry skin meant so much
to me
to you
to us.
I loved you for skin so white
it seemed to pulse with life.
You loved me for my skin so brown
it made your liberalism authentic.

your public pictures show impossible worlds
for me
for you
for us.
Your white daughter from your white husband
makes the edges of absence hurt
      she looks like you,
             I'm sure you know.
That Santa Clarita house is bigger than both our parents'
combined.
By the way,
your husband looks like me,
           a me I couldn't be
            I'm sure now
                you know: successful.
I wonder if your heart would clinch at how often I argue
now
for workers,
for minorities,
for hope.

for choosing to be selfless instead of successful
for choosing the life you idolized
but one you'd have to work at,
where I slip into it like a second skin.

I'm sorry my struggles made me hate whiteness.
I'm sorry my struggles made you hate brownness.
I'm sorry I won't try to friend you
because that little girl
        who looks so much like you
is impossible.

Sculpting Identity

Sculpting an identity in Old Sacramento
amongst the retired trains—this is not a metaphor
From hindsight, I could see through the fog of my own assery
the three months I failed at living in this city.
I moved for a girl
I moved for escape
I moved because I wanted
and wanted
and wanted
and I failed for fear.

I'm walking my old haunts now on break
I'm only visiting who I was
after performing who I am at a conference.
My coworkers keep a tally of the things I negate:
warm beverages
Sacramento
people
people
people
and I feel so uncomfortable and awkward
with who I was lingering over my shoulder

They can't see my negatives for what they tell—
only hindsight gives me perspective—
I am the product of racially opposed parents
who didn't have the words to talk about
all the things that would have helped me succeed
the past
race
people
love
love
love

never time to stop working
never time to learn so many languages.

The Quivering Shame of Dim Remembrance
for Richard Anthony Beaver

The day after election day
nearly a decade ago
was the first day I awoke
without you in the world
I had to shower for the first time
without you in the world
wash away the paralyzing grief
so that I could go about my day
as though it were any other day
and the days have become easier
to get through, the occasional grief
more of an empty drawer
where knives were once kept
the longest lacerations coming with firsts
the first taquito eaten in your honor
the first rev of a Porsche engine
knowing you weren't behind the wheel
the first donation to Stand Up 2 Cancer
knowing it was too late to help you
the first Kings game without you
the Kings first Stanley Cup
unable to celebrate with you
and I worry that I have not grieved enough
that I don't think of you enough
that my memories of you have grown too dim

but I know too that I'm not yet done with firsts
that there will be times the thought of you
will sneak up on me and with it
the momentarily paralyzing grief
followed by the smile
the warmth of heart
and sometimes the laughter
that accompanies my memories
of your life

The Girl Could Play Music

In silence,
Mom commutes two hours
    each way.
She spends hours in her head
because, or so I've been told,
she grew up in a house filled with notes
with family gatherings loaded with love and laughs
and music,
    my god
        the music
all centering around a sister and her guitar
her piano
sometimes even a clarinet,
a sister who strung the family together like a melody.
And when she left,
silence broke.

The quiet washed away my grandfather's presence,
my uncle's laughter,
my grandmother's sanity,
my mom's childhood.
When the sister ran away,
she took with her
all the sound in the world.

The late night call

Grandma's gone…

…

Her heart burst…

…

She slumped over in the nurse's arms…

…

It was quick…

…

She didn't suffer…

…

…

…

How's work going?

Disneyland to San Francisco to LA to Hawai'i to San Pedro, San Pedro, Nowhere

Let's Celebrate Terror

Parades and fireworks scare me.
The regimented lines
precise formations
are meant to strike fear in the enemy.
They say, look at us,
we are trained
disciplined
mighty.
Even at Disneyland, the bubbly lighted floats
are separated by brightly colored soldiers
marching bands sounding triumphant.
The show will be followed by explosions in the sky.
The thing that makes it enjoyable is the absence of shrapnel
the physical casualties
easy victory.
I get the appeal of parades,
but in the face of that unity and organization,
I see written, in huge black and white letters:
"WOE TO YOU IF YOU BECOME MY ENEMY"
and I wonder what rule I'll violate to change my status.

Ironic weight

When I left the church
I made my name ironic
There's nothing wrong with the church
I just feel that
if my neighbor suffers
I am a sinner

preparations for parenthood

the potted red ti leaf plant
smuggled from Hawai'i
and given to me by a friend
because of the little care it needs
to grow and flourish
withered and died

With the Tall Boys

Some days, the sun sends invitations,
it makes the grass seem softer.
Some days, the shade brings a cold
that reaches into the bones
and only light can bring warmth.
Those days tug at the corners of your mouth.

On those days your parks are filled with those
turned out of shelters and halfway houses.
They sit and sip their pan-handled tall boys
and admire the world.

A young couple pushes a stroller through
them, a wrapper slips from the father's hand as
a dog runs up barking at the interlopers.
They laugh because it's cute.

A tall boy sipper says,
"Those assholes just littered."
As the dog sinks its teeth into the baby's leg
pulls and pulls. Tugs and tugs.

The parents scream and kick the small dog
away, The baby cries.
The homeless man smiles
because the sun's invitation,
the soft grass,
the warmth in your bones,
are also promises of burns
sores
and breaks

Saint Peter, Let Me In

If it'd do any good,
I'd stand in the street pronouncing my love for him
but that spot's taken by the crackhead,
no, not the one you're thinking of,
the other one that blows kisses.
The one you're thinking of died last week
in an alley off Pacific.

If it'd do any good,
I'd put an ad in the paper,
filled with verse Fante would shake a fist at,
words to make the great Bukowski nod
but ads cost money
and he don't read.

If it'd do any good,
I'd write it in his language,
write it in the jagged RSP print,
in Croatian and Italian
in English and Spanish
in omelets and sandwiches
in the pepperoni on a pizza.

But I know it won't
already
it won't.
At best he'll let me in
with a sideways glare;
he has learned to trust
only the things that stay
and never hope.

To Build on Fire

My feet itch to get San Francisco under them,
my brain burns with competition.
You told me you're moving there.
"It's got culture," you said.
"It has history."
So does LA, I said.
As I pass the late night streetwalkers
and their "be safe" whispers,
two homeless men fighting over a burner
amongst countless homeless fighting for space,
a polite argument at Walgreens over a woman's last $3,
and tourists, tourists, tourists,
I compare the only thing that matters:
what you do with the ashes.

You see, San Francisco measures time in quakes and fires.
Its history marks those points when nature clears the board,
And the city gathers the ashes,
rebuilds
makes better.
It's a city that uses the fire to renew and conserve.

Los Angeles measures time in land grabs and fires,
the fires of frustration and fury.
It doesn't wait for nature,
No,

It's always burning,
always angry
because this city doesn't rebuild,
it sells itself
whether it's the expansion of the westside
to Japanese invasion in the eighties
to the Chinese now,
gentrification and white flight.
This city is always burning,
And like the late night
streetwalkers, LA tucks in
all the Angelenos and
whispers:
"Be safe."

Night and Anger in Los Angeles

Remember that night I was lost in LA
how late it was when we'd left the Pantages
how hungry we were because
we hadn't had time to eat
always in a rush we were back then
and really no different now
always in a rush and always hungry
your grandfather had just died
you were angry
angry about it being so late
angry about being hungry
angry about me being lost
it wasn't the first time
LA encouraged our darker sides
you angry and
I lost and night
so completely descended.

I'm in LA again and it's late
those memories have come back
after a long absence
as though they were stuck
in this place
awaiting my return,
as though they belong
more to the city
than to me

the memories have done nothing
more than remind me that it's even later
and I'm still lost and searching for something
that will make sense of everything
will make the anger and the night subside.

Neutral Milk Hotel

It's like the Muppet Show,
a band of misfits with unique styles
voices
sounds and combinations,
a cacophony around a calming center.
Its heart is an earnest voice
coordinating the chaos.

I love the parts when Kermit,
from frustration,
loses his shit at his crew.

Only, what if Kermit's rages are not
from irritation
but a call for something his friends
        at times
lack
a feeling we
        all too often
lack
what if Kermit is screaming for you to see
the little girl not watching TV
because she's curled in an upstairs room
quiet and still
in fear of real monsters.

Kermit,
like a too fragile singer in a folk band,
knows the only way
is empathy
and his rage reminds us
we are always lost.

Basquiat: *CPRKR,* 1982

the bird sings
his brass song
improvising
the world
creating
anew
from the ashes
of history
awakening us
to the moment
to our place
in a new history
called the present
where it's not
too late
yet

Hawaiian Homes Revisited: 10 Days On Maui

10 days left:
The first day, kona winds so bad
the governor closes the schools.
We argue, Nani and I, about living on Maui
in her grandfather's house
on the Hawaiian rez
  eating fruit and playing ukulele
  instead of fry bread and drums.
It's a familiar argument:
feeling authentic on one side
feeling familiar on the other.

9 days left:
With the winds
no activity in the harbor.
Protect your property mode.
The neighbors next door are new,
and, to outward appearances,
broken.
White husband greets me from his porch
baby in one hand
beer in the other.
We never see his wife
Nani wonders if the previous neighbors had died
  She says "50%ers are getting old, you see,
  They're dying off
  and you need 50% to win Hawaiian land."

She says "Race is a number.
And I'm too far
from a whole
one."

8 days left:
We see a sailboat planted in the sandbar
High winds and low tide;
it had broken away.
Her grandfather's truck
has malfunctioning speedometer, gas gauge,
radio,
and emergency brake,
It's only comfortable in first and third gear
with no heart for smoothness.
I say, "but the clock ticks away just fine"
"It does," she agrees, "it does."

7 days left:
We avoid the beach and the ship
like we avoid luaus and fire knife dances,
the imported authentic
The queen lost her throne one hundred years before,
surrendered to rich white families.
She called them teachers, classmates, husband.
I call them friends, cousin, mom.
We go to a petition rally for a constitutional convention
The natives need to keep whatever rights they have left.
An hour in,
the rally hasn't started.

The organizer forgot the petition at home.
Nani signs the back of a flyer

6 days left:
We stay on the beach most of the day
with a bag of marinating chicken
a bag of charcoal
a bag of books.
From time to time, we watch the ship
creep closer to the shoreline with each passing tide.
I say, "That can be us."
She says "I'm not getting stuck here."

5 days left:
I look for a job at the local college
"just for kicks."
She says "And I'll find one at the library."
We both return with nothing,
nothing but hope
hope and the possibility of being,
like the ship, stranded on the beach,
living in a tent,
off the land
until a tourist finds us dirty and asks we be removed.

I smile. "At least we'll have each other."
She says, "Just each other doesn't add up to a living,
but it does sum up divorce."

4 days left:
We drive through Lahaina's one strip,
Passing the ship, now pressed against the seawall.
She says "we lost this land and it's never coming back."
I say "no, it's not.
But maybe we can make it better."
She asks, "What's better than paradise?"

3 days left:
The ship has been cut into pieces,
lifted by crane from off the sea wall.
It's been barely a year since our first visit.
The promise of self-sufficiency
at the start of Hawaiian homestead
seems
fleeting.
Her uncle's girlfriend across the street
has more tenants than family living with her,
but the grass is so green
the hibiscus fragrant.
Nani asks "What should we carry home with us?"
I answer "everything. I want it all."
She says "I'm sorry, love. We can't afford the baggage fee."

2 days left:
The ship is not even stranded or salvaged.
The pieces are left on the road:
three large chunks.

The locals come at night
pick it clean
leave nothing of value by morning
and even less by the next day
"Do you want a souvenir?"

The last day:
We hunt for the dream of Hawaii to take home with us,
not the tourist one
with the imported sandy beach
or the coconut bras from Tahiti;
instead, we look for the familiar
for slippers piled in front of a house,
for poi in a calabash bowl
for the dream that the country we are part of
will make this right.

Higher Plateaus

"Every generation has the obligation to free men's minds for a look at new worlds. . . to look out from a higher plateau than the last generation."
—Ellison S. Onizuka

Standing at the gravesite of Ellison Onizuka
in Punchbowl Cemetery Oahu
I think back on that fateful day
when the unthinkable happened
waiting after the morning bell had rung
for the teacher to let us in
waiting. . . waiting. . . waiting. . .
never dreaming what was waiting for us
on the other side of that door
watching the news the rest of the day
seeing the shuttle lift off in a cloud of white
seeing the flash of orange and yellow
hearing the cheers fade to breathlessness
an awe-inspiring scene in one swift moment
turning into something awful

knowing later that Ellison
survived the initial blast
at least long enough
to activate his air pack
which may have given him
a few extra moments
a few extra breaths
before oxygen
was no longer available
before consciousness
was no longer available

and I wonder what wonder there was in those final moments
thoughts perhaps of a comet left unexamined for the time being
of the confines of creativity, the circumference of imagination
the continual frustration of human aspiration
or great amazement at this small step created in earth's
    atmosphere
this grand failure that burned a symbol in the sky
pointing to where humanity was headed next
recognition that where he left off, another would pick up
and expand the limits of human consciousness
expand the limits of human understanding
just a little more until the next grand failure

There Are Projects Across the Street from Mark Twain's Grave in Elmira

I pass them, watching kids play in the cool afternoon,
never lingering too far from their units,
never straying too far into the flat,
empty spaces between apartment buildings
that look like the ones I just drove from in NYC,
the ones I lived next to in Compton,
the ones I live near in San Pedro,
boxed and stacked units separated from each other
by weird stretches of no man's land grass,
a place where battles for space and progress are fought.
These kids seem to be the only ones with enough sense
not to step out of their lane,
but that's the point, isn't it?
Is Samuel Clemens laughing through this eternal second?
After hundreds of pages, his country,
my country,
still doesn't see the worth in its people,
the wonder of creation,
and everything that we lose for not seeing.

Sunny Side Up

At the corner of Powell Street
and O'Farrell he stopped to listen
to the sax player out of courtesy;
he would never stop for the street
musicians but, head down,
would walk with purpose
toward his task;
he wasn't sure what made him
stop
now
until he stopped
thinking about stopping
  about walking
  about his task
and listened
to the music
to the notes
climbing one by one
to his ears
and then his heart
and then his finger tips
and knees and toes
until the music stopped
and he woke up
and the next song started
but without the same effect;
and he started to walk again
and think again

and wonder what that feeling was
and wonder what that music was
and wonder when he'd wondered last.

He came back to the same spot
at the same time the next day
and waited for the same song
to evoke the same feeling
but it never came,
so he threw some change
in the sax case
and walked away.

He tried again the next day
and had to wait a while
before he heard the song again,
and he closed his eyes
and the feeling came back again;
he felt his mouth form a smile.
when the song ended,
he walked up to the street musician
and asked what the song
was called.
"man, that's Sunny Side Up," he said,
"wrote that one myself."
he dropped a five dollar bill
in the sax case
and walked away down Powell Street.

The next day he waited
for a song to end
and asked the musician
to play Sunny Side Up.
"you got it, man," he said,
and went into it
sending those notes back
to his ears, his heart,
his fingers and knees and toes.

Every day he'd ask the street musician
to play Sunny Side Up
and every day he'd drop
a five into the sax case
until the day the musician
wasn't on the corner
of Powell and O'Farrell
and there he stood
in the empty space,
wondering,
before he started walking again
with his head down
with purpose
toward his
task.

San Pedro, Let Me In

I want to be an arrival that never departs.
I want to see everyone
eventually
leave.
I want to feel anger, regret,
and pride with their absence.
I can't forget the pride
because I can plant roots in a place where few others
do and thrive.
I can wear the word "ghetto" like a badge
because it hides the values I hold:
family, loyalty, local.
I can be like you,
small in the face of big,
small but enough.

In the shadow of future dreams

is a life tilting toward oblivion
    with a dying grandmother
        and her dying memory
            who recognized that she recognized me
    but had no idea who I was
               half the time

    and a grandfather
        who yelled and screamed
            and threatened everything with fists
        that were probably too slow to threaten anything
    who provided me a model of what it meant
                 to be Italian American
    and who, when my grandmother died,
           discovered he had nothing left to fight for
           and let his guard down to death

    and an uncle
        who proved that too young to die
           is a human construct with no basis in reality
             because dying young is not an exception
        but the basis for living young
             for however long life might last
        to never lose the sense of wonder
           that the truly young possess

because bombs are real
    because severed
        limbs
  and severed
      lives
           are real

even if we only see them on television
even if we refuse to speak out against
them

even if we value our own lives
and the lives of our imagined
communities
more than the lives we destroy
with our complicit silence

because drones really do lurk
in the shadows of the night
in the shadows of broad daylight
in the shadows of our unconscious
minds
in the darkness of our conscious
minds
where there are no shadows
in lands far enough away
where we cannot see the shadows
in lands where there are no children
because who can live in such a land
and remain a child

except sunlight is not hard
to capture in a box
if you remember how to dream

and moonlight will stay
in a bottle without the need
for a cap
out how imagination works   if you figure

The Shadow of What We Were

There is a house in downtown San Pedro,
dilapidated and crumbling
with an impossible staircase leading up to it.
The house sits on a patch of land that rises,
like a chicken pock scar on a meth head,
it's foundation is level with the roofs of the buildings around it.
Romee tells me, it's from before they leveled the hill for the bars,
the lumber
the shipping
the Navy.
She says, this was downhill before they carved out Beacon
street.
And the city carries its memories in its genes.
San Pedro remembers its lawlessness,
it remembers its bars and whorehouses
and it screams its memories uphill—
wherever there is an uphill—
Remember! Remember when the bar owners, the people who
        made the money,
lived up hill because the drunks would be too tired to make it
        to bug them off hours.
Remember! Remember when, as they got more money, they
        moved further up hill
away from their bars,
the port,
the drunks,
the whores,
their customers.

Remember! Remember they kept the houses nearby to own
    everything,
to rent you space, a stool, an apartment
morning, noon, and night.
Listen, and the land says "there used to be a cliffs here for a
    reason:
go too far, and you'll fall off the earth".

A Safeway in San Francisco

It's my turn to dream, Allen Ginsberg, as I walk the streets of Chinatown, North Beach, to the Embarcadero, bus back to the Richmond as the sun descends again, and the fog descends again on the city and the minds that inhabit it.

I walk into a supermarket as much in need of images as you were once to appease the appetite, appease the howling hunger for something fresh, the kiwis rotting on the shelf, mold growing on the papayas, too sweet the smell of the strawberries.

Stop hiding in the bananas, Allen Ginsberg, with your prick tied to a bunch, hoping the young boys will unwittingly grab it in their hunger for something out of reach, the young boys will come when they are ready, old man.

When did possibilities turn into dreams and what has become of dreams now?

Walk with me out into America, out into the dark night, in this time of the ostrich, now is our time or we have no time, your time has not passed though you be but a ghostly dream, I will not let you lie quiet while there is work still to be done.

The smog is still there, the industrial clamor of capitalism which almost ruined America is still there, escaped unscathed but being propped up now by the living corpses of the people, the people, yes, with their heads buried.

What America is still possible? What dreams do we still allow ourselves?

139

A Pedro Death

I want to die here
in the first earth I purchased
on ground I claim as mine
        but don't own.

I want to die here
in a city where you need generations of credentials for an opinion
and I have none.

I want to die here
like I lived here
always on the outside
always wanting

So bury me when the weight of want breaks my body
on that hill next to Bukowski
and his written warning: "Don't Try."

Bury me to show him it was
always about the attempt
show him that success is only given to fools
who confuse luck for accomplishment.

Bury me in San Pedro
because I'm too stubborn to fall elsewhere
and too smart to think
I can have what I want.

Acknowledgements

Thank you to Anna Lozada for providing the incredible cover art.

Nothing but gratitude for the editors of the following journals, websites, and anthologies who published these poems or versions of them:

Basquiat: *CPRKR*, 1982 – *Cadence Collective*
Basquiat: *Untitled (Black Tar and Feathers)*, 1982 – *Cadence Collective*
Basquiat: *Untitled (Life Study)*, 1983 – *Short Poems Ain't Got Nobody to Love (Anthology)*
Breathing in Reverse – *Cadence Collective*
A Circus for the Elderly – *Missing Persons: reflections on dementia*
The Fighter – *Drunk Monkeys*
A Grandmother with Dementia Remembers – *Drunk Monkeys*
Hawaiian Homes Revisited – *Spot Lit 2016*
Hunger is a Snowflake – *Gutters and Alleyways: Perspectives on Poverty and Struggle*
I guess it's easier to just do white (published as I've gotten by this long without it) – *Cadence Collective*
the lean mad days – *Dead Snakes*
Plastic Spatulas – *Spot Lit 2016*
A Safeway in San Francisco – *Chiron Review, Issue #99*
Son of a Scab – *Blue Collar Review*
The Square Root of Poverty – *Cadence Collective*

About the Authors

Christian Hanz Lozada is the author of the photographic history book Hawaiians in Los Angeles. He lives in an insanely small house in San Pedro, CA, with his wife, Lessa, who kicks way more ass than he does, a dog unironically named Maka, a cat ironically named Oliver Ricky Baker Lozada, and a single fish named Teddy of various breeds. He teaches his neighbors' kids at Los Angeles Harbor College. In all his experience, he has learned love is the promise of loss, and there are but two reactions to this fact: clutch tighter your loves or push them away. Christian always chooses to push.

Steven Hendrix began writing poetry modeled on the 19th century British Romantics. Once he realized he wasn't living in the 19th century, he found a more contemporary style for his poetry. He received his M.A. in English and Comparative Literature from California State University, Long Beach. He currently lives in an insanely expensive apartment in San Francisco, CA, with his wife Erin and son Langston. He likes to end his readings with a maxim appropriated from his professor and friend Ray Lacoste: Be kind to each other. It's the last revolutionary act left.

Christian and Steven met while working together at Borders Book Store in Costa Mesa, CA. They began sharing the same space to write on a weekly basis, then monthly, then whenever they could find the time. But after all the years of talking about their writing together, reading each other's writing, and providing each other feedback, they realized they were writing about a lot of the same themes. In 2015, they ran the pop-up bookstore and reading series Read on Till Morning in San Pedro, CA, primarily focusing on local writers and small presses.

"Too often, class and poverty are ignored in writing about life in America and specifically in the diaspora that leads people to California. *Leave With More Than You Came With* is a moving odyssey of mixed-race and multi-ethnic working-class families through other displaced communities. In this collection of fine poems, we travel through the South, Hawai'i, San Francisco and end in San Pedro, "on the hill next to Bukowski." A must-read for anyone who wants to understand the longings of those who come to the Pacific West."
—**Naomi Hirahara**, Edgar Award-winning author of the Mas Arai mystery series and co-author of *Terminal Island: The Lost Communities of Los Angeles Harbor.*

"Christian Lozada and Steve Hendrix aim to help you leave with more than you came with. Through the process of coming to terms with the years that must be forgotten, these poems offer geographic lessons and explain why we are all immigrants. Circling the South Bay and San Pedro and over the ocean to Maui, Lozada and Hendrix grapple with racism, dementia, and identity in order to transform worry and doubt into a book of beauty."
—**Mike Sonksen**, author of *Letters to My City*

"I've read better."
—**Mark Twain**, author of *Tom Sawyer Abroad* and *Tom Sawyer, Detective*

Made in USA - Kendallville, IN
1066889_9781095407264
04.02.2020 0752